free to DREAM

AF241840

Titilayo Akinniyi

free to DREAM

Copyright © 2020 by Titilayo Akinniyi

All rights reserved.

This book or any portion thereof may not be

reproduced or used in any manner

whatsoever without the express written

permission of the publisher except for the

use of brief quotations in a book review.

Paperback ISBN: 978-1-9992310-1-9

eBook ISBN: 978-1-9992310-2-6

Unless otherwise indicated,

all scripture references are

from the New King James Version

To order additional copies of this book, contact:

The 360 Degree Woman

Website: https://the360degreewoman.org/

Email: info@the360degreewoman.org

free to DREAM

Acknowledgement

All the glory, power, praise and honour belong to God, the giver of dreams. He is the one and only God who fulfils His divine plan and purpose in the lives of His children.

Thank You Father, for giving me your divine inspiration for this work.

I will forever be grateful to you Lord.

My ever-caring husband and helper of my destiny, Engineer Olusegun Akinniyi. You are the principal instrument used by God for the fulfilment of many of my dreams.

Thank you.

My Princesses – Oluwakemi and Olayinka Akinniyi. The Prince in the house, Olusegun Oluwatobiloba Akinniyi. I celebrate God's grace in your lives.

free to DREAM

You are always there to support your dad and myself in prayer. I will never forget the role you all played while trusting God for the grace to relocate to the United Kingdom. Your prayer of agreement worked wonders to the point of our friends calling the three of you angels in prayer of agreement.

Pastor Chinedu, I am very grateful for the insight given to my family to use the words of God to bring to pass His purpose in our lives. You showed us the power of the shout of GRACE GRACE.

Sister Moji Oladimeji my prayer partner, my sister in Christ and great supporter of God's grace in my life, thank you so much. Together, we attended many prayer meetings at Christ Living Spring Apostolic Ministry (CLAM) to seek God's face and favour.

Thank you so much for the quality time you invested to make this book a success.

free to DREAM

You all made my life so easy and beautiful.

I greatly appreciate you all for your support.

Great success and honour shall be yours in

Jesus name.

free to DREAM

Dedication

This book is dedicated to The Almighty God, The giver of great dreams. The only God who says a thing and brings it to pass.

And to everyone out there who broke through the limitations or fear created by the situations or circumstances around them and dared to dream and work out the fulfilment of their dreams with total trust in God.

To everyone with a dream and who is praying for their dreams to come to realisation, I would like to say, "keep dreaming". One day, your story will become an inspiration to others.

free to DREAM

Table of Contents

free to DREAM

free to DREAM

INTRODUCTION

Life events start with a dream. Call it imagination, if you like. Everything in existence started as a thought or dream in the mind of someone. There is always a picture of a thing or event before they become visible or physical. The world that we live in today is a product of God's vision or dream. As humans, we have great dreams. We dream to have a great future and become great in life. Some of our dreams, life visions or ambitions sometimes appear to us as if they are too big to achieve. But the truth is that dreams cost nothing. You need no money to dream. All you need is your mind and yourself. You do not have to hire or employ anyone to dream your dream for you. This is because nobody knows you better than you. Nobody knows the feelings that you have or your ambitions in life. Nobody can interpret

free to DREAM

your inner picture better than yourself. In short, no one can live your life for you.

Our identity or picture is revealed in the scripture which describes us as people with the spirit of excellence, having dominion over everything created by God and having no lack of anything good. We are a people with the capacity to create and command a thing and bring it to pass. We are made in the perfect image and likeness of God. We are a people who have been set free by God never to experience any form of bondage. This is the dream and plan of God for everyone created in His image. There is no room for mediocrity. When we fall short of God's plan for us, we become real failures in life. As humans, we naturally crave for success and comfort in life. We want to be great in life and to be valued as human beings.

free to DREAM

But what is it that makes people leave their comfortable homes or nations to go to another man's country? Man is always looking for a way to fulfill his dreams on earth.

WHAT IS A DREAM?

A dream is an expression of your inner desire. It is your imagination of possibilities even when those possibilities seem impossible.

In the context of this book, we shall be looking at dreams as your thoughts, your cherished ambitions, your cravings, the image you see with your mind's eye, your fantasies, your aspirations, your wishes, your hopes, the things you long for or the ideas that form in your mind.

A dream costs you nothing. The only thing you need to dream is you and your mind. To dream is not illegal. To dream is powerful. To dream has no limitations. In your dream, you can travel the world round without any financial cost. You can bring anything to be as true, in the power of your dream.

free to DREAM

A dream that is aligned with God's plan and recognises the power of God in its fulfilment always comes to pass. Joseph dreamt of greatness according to the plan and purpose of God and he saw it come to pass.

In Genesis 14, God told Abraham that whatsoever he could see would be given to him. To what extent could Abraham see with his physical eyes? How tall was Abraham that he could see beyond the present situation? He engaged in the power of dreams. He imagined what he truly desired and what he really wanted to see in his life. God promised to make him the father of nations and a channel of blessings to many. He saw it in his imagination, and it came to pass.

Do not engage in unprofitable dreams or vain dreams. Be conscious of the relevance of your dream to the kingdom of God. What is the relevance of your dream to humanity? Is it just

free to DREAM

for your benefit and that of your family? Someone said, if all the wealth you have can only take care of your family, then, you need to ask for more. Great wealth is not for one person or one family. It is a great thing when many can benefit from your wealth.

Joseph's dream looked like it was just for him to become a leader among his family, but God's plan was beyond Joseph and his family. As a matter of fact, it was beyond the tribe of Israel and was meant for all nations and all generations - both Jews and Greeks. Through Joseph, Jacob and his sons were preserved as a nation through whom the Saviour of the world would be born. Also, the nation of Egypt was preserved through the gift of interpretation of dreams that God gave to Joseph.

Dare to dream big and allow God to demonstrate his power and greatness in fulfilling the dreams He revealed to you. Your aspirations in life could emanate from a dream or what The Holy Spirit caused you to see in a vision of the night.

TYPES OF DREAMS

There are three types of dreams depending on where the inspiration for the dream derives from.

1. Self-inspired dreams
2. God-inspired dreams
3. Devil-inspired dreams

Self-inspired dreams

Sometimes we imagine who we would like to become or events that we would like to happen in our lives. As human beings, I believe God has deposited in us, some basic life desires no matter who we are or, where we are. We long for good life. Our souls long for positive

free to DREAM

happenings in our lives. No man would wake up in the morning and start to pray for lack and want, or desire to be at the bottom of the corporate ladder. We are creations of the Most High God with His Spirit in us. This makes us want to experience the best in life. The bible says that God breathed the breath of life into man after forming him and the lifeless creation became a living being. Also, God said, let us create man in our image and the likeness of God.

Genesis 1:26-27

26 Then God said, "Let Us make man in Our image, according to Our likeness; let them have dominion over the fish of the sea, over the birds of the air, and over the cattle, over all the earth and over every creeping thing that creeps on the earth."

free to DREAM

27 So God created man in His own image; in the image of God He created him; male and female He created them.

This means that the excellent spirit at work in God, works in us too.

What happened along the way that made your dream to become a thing of the past? The word of God tells us that 'while men slept, the enemy came and sowed tares among the wheat'.

Matthew 13:25

25 But while men slept, his enemy came and sowed tares among the wheat, and went his way.

Today, the enemy is having a field day planting tares of lack, want, barrenness and negative happenings in people's lives while they are spiritually asleep instead of watching prayerfully, to bring to pass all that God has deposited in them at creation. Spiritual slumber

free to DREAM

gives the enemy an opportunity to disrupt the plan of God in our lives. Sleep makes us powerless. To be who God wants us to be, we need to be spiritually awake. The physical is controlled by the spiritual. Our connection to God is something that should not be treated lightly. Our spiritual muscles must be properly developed to stand the test of life. Good life is not meant for the spiritually weak. The enemy is moving to and fro, looking for whom he may devour. You simply cannot afford to go on spiritual vacation. To go on holiday spiritually is an invitation to dream destroyers.

1 Peter 5:8

8 Be sober, be vigilant; because your adversary the devil walks about like a roaring lion, seeking whom he may devour.

Luke18:1

1 Then He spoke a parable to them, that men always ought to pray and not lose heart,

free to DREAM

The dream of every man is to become somebody in life. No man ever dreams of becoming nobody in life. Every time a man's experience differs from his dream, he becomes agitated and starts to search for his identity. He is faced with an identity crisis and is not sure who he really is any more. He redirects his time and energy trying to be like this person or that person. Sometimes it pays off, but most times we cast a 'perfect picture' in our minds that ultimately leads us astray and causes us to miss our destiny altogether.

If you do not know where you are going, or God's plan for your life, every road will look like the road to your destination. Every business will look like your breakthrough business. Everybody needs to seek God's face for the perfect direction in order to be successful in the journey of life. Outside God's perfect will is endless struggle and waste of God-given time. That shall not be your portion in Jesus name.

free to DREAM

God-inspired dreams

God-inspired dreams are those dreams that reveal to you the purpose of God for your life. Such dreams are fully packed with what God has for you and consistently lead you in the right path. When God shows you your destination and how to get there, no matter your situation or the storm around you, one thing will keep you going, and that thing is the God-inspired dream. For sure, His word will back up the dream and provide confirmation that the dream is from Him. Dreams like these can only be fulfilled by Him alone. Applying human efforts to bring it to pass may lead to frustration in life. Running to achieve this by your own strength will only lead to a burn-out. If it is from God, achieving the dream will be stress free. The fulfilment of God inspired dreams happen in God's own time.

free to DREAM

Joseph's dreams were for an appointed time. He was only a teenager when God revealed his destiny to him, but the dream was not fulfilled until he was around 30.

In Genesis 37:9, he dreamt that the sun, the moon and 11 stars bowed down to him suggesting that he would be a ruler over his parents and brothers.

Genesis 37:9

9 Then he dreamed still another dream and told it to his brothers, and said, "Look, I have dreamed another dream. And this time, the sun, the moon, and the eleven stars bowed down to me."

Here is what happened in Genesis 43:28. The brothers said, Thy servant our father is in good health.

Joseph's brothers referred to their father as a servant of Joseph. This was a fulfilment of the

free to DREAM

dream that Joseph had in chapter 37. When your dream is God-inspired, it will surely be fulfilled. It may take a long or short time. All you need do is wait for it.

Though it tarries, wait for it because it will not tarry. It may seem long or appear as if it will not come to pass. But hold on to God and His word. God is never late to fulfil His promises to His children.

Habakkuk 2:3

For the vision is yet for an appointed time;

But at the end it will speak, and it will not lie.

Though it tarries, wait for it;

Because it will surely come,

It will not tarry.

God allowed some kings in the bible to dream so He could promote His kingdom and His children. Two classic examples are the dreams

free to DREAM

of king Pharaoh in Genesis 41 and Nebuchadnezzar in Daniel 4:5

A dream inspired by God must have the kingdom of God and people as its focus.

Devil-inspired dreams

Any dream that does not seek the good of others or that is centred solely on self is not Godly. Neither is a dream that seeks to make others feel bad about who they are or that makes their situation worse. The bible says that the imagination of man is desperately wicked.

A dream that seeks to destroy other people's destinies is devil-inspired. Pray against it.

Jeremiah 17:9

9 "The heart is deceitful above all things,

And desperately wicked;

Who can know it?

free to DREAM

BIBLICAL EXAMPLES OF DREAMS

The secret things of God or His plans are revealed sometimes through dreams. In Genesis 28:12-15, God revealed Himself to Jacob and showed him what the future held for him.

Genesis 28:12-15

12 Then he dreamed, and behold, a ladder was set up on the earth, and its top reached to heaven; and there the angels of God were ascending and descending on it.

13 And behold, the Lord stood above it and said: "I am the Lord God of Abraham your father and the God of Isaac; the land on which you lie I will give to you and your descendants. 14 Also your descendants shall be as the dust of the earth; you shall spread abroad to the west and the east, to the north and the south; and in

free to DREAM

you and in your seed all the families of the earth shall be blessed.

15 Behold, I am with you and will keep you wherever you go, and will bring you back to this land; for I will not leave you until I have done what I have spoken to you."

God's impending punishment on the household of king Abimelech was revealed to the king through a dream.

Genesis 20:3

3 But God came to Abimelech in a dream by night, and said to him, "Indeed you are a dead man because of the woman whom you have taken, for she is a man's wife."

Joseph dreamt of his position in destiny.

Genesis 37:5-8

free to DREAM

5 Now Joseph had a dream, and he told it to his brothers; and they hated him even more.

6 So he said to them, "Please hear this dream which I have dreamed:

7 There we were, binding sheaves in the field. Then behold, my sheaf arose and also stood upright; and indeed, your sheaves stood all around and bowed down to my sheaf."

8 And his brothers said to him, "Shall you indeed reign over us? Or shall you indeed have dominion over us?" So, they hated him even more for his dreams and for his words.

Joseph's ability to interpret Pharaoh's dream paved the way for him to become the Prime Minister in a foreign land.

God revealed to Pharaoh the famine that was to happen in Egypt, how to be prepared for it and how to make room for excess.

Genesis 41:38-42

free to DREAM

38 And Pharaoh said to his servants, "Can we find such a one as this, a man in whom is the Spirit of God?"

39 Then Pharaoh said to Joseph, "Inasmuch as God has shown you all this, there is no one as discerning and wise as you.

40 You shall be over my house, and all my people shall be ruled according to your word; only in regard to the throne will I be greater than you."

41 And Pharaoh said to Joseph, "See, I have set you over all the land of Egypt."

42 Then Pharaoh took his signet ring off his hand and put it on Joseph's hand; and he clothed him in garments of fine linen and put a gold chain around his neck.

His ability to interpret king Nebuchadnezzar's dream made Daniel to become relevant to many generations.

free to DREAM

Daniel 4:19

19 Then Daniel, whose name was Belteshazzar, was astonished for a time, and his thoughts troubled him. So the king spoke, and said, "Belteshazzar, do not let the dream or its interpretation trouble you."

Belteshazzar answered and said, "My lord, may the dream concern those who hate you, and its interpretation concern your enemies!

Daniel 5:12

12 Inasmuch as an excellent spirit, knowledge, understanding, interpreting dreams, solving riddles, and explaining enigmas were found in this Daniel, whom the king named Belteshazzar, now let Daniel be called, and he will give the interpretation."

The birth of Jesus was revealed to His earthly father, Joseph through a dream.

Matthew 1:20

free to DREAM

20 But while he thought about these things, behold, an angel of the Lord appeared to him in a dream, saying, "Joseph, son of David, do not be afraid to take to you Mary your wife, for that which is conceived in her is of the Holy Spirit.

The escape from king Herod who wanted to kill Jesu when he was a baby was revealed to Joseph in a dream.

Matthew 2:12

12 Then, being divinely warned in a dream that they should not return to Herod, they departed for their own country another way.

ENEMIES OF YOUR DREAM

Dream stoppers

The moment you tell some people about your dream, they start to look for ways to stop it. They are not comfortable with your dreams. Beware of such people. All they have to offer you are negative stories of how someone somewhere had such a dream and it never came to pass. They make you feel too small for your dreams and go to great lengths to explain why you are too unqualified for such dreams because of your gender, colour, family background or even your past to mention a few. They help to create barriers within you, and all you want to do is to cast off the reality of your dreams. Beware of such people. They may even be your close family or friends. Nurture your dream and table it before God.

free to DREAM

Dream haters

These set of people hate you because of your dreams. Your dream is making them to feel very uncomfortable and all they think about is how to eliminate you and your dream. You do not have to offend them before they hate you. They do not want anything that looks like success around you. Hatred is acidic. It is blindfolding and your haters do not care about the benefit of your dream to you or anyone, neither do they care who you are or what your dream is about.

Genesis 37:5

5 Now Joseph had a dream, and he told it to his brothers; and they hated him even more.

Dream slayers or killers

These are people who do not want your dream to see the light of day. They either help you to

free to DREAM

abort it or kill it as soon as it is delivered. Seeing your dreams come to pass makes them feel uncomfortable. It suffocates them. It makes them want to get rid of you so that your dream will die as soon as you are out of the way.

You can dream as much as you want, but these people will make sure that you do not live to see the dream fulfilled. Talk about the wickedness of men.

Genesis 37:18-20

18 Now when they saw him afar off, even before he came near them, they conspired against him to kill him.

19 Then they said to one another, "Look, this dreamer is coming!

20 Come therefore, let us now kill him and cast him into some pit; and we shall say, 'Some wild

free to DREAM

beast has devoured him.' We shall see what will become of his dreams!"

Dream snatchers/betrayers

As soon as you share your dream with dream snatchers, they start thinking of how to take over your dream and make it theirs. They may be supportive initially to study how well you are building up the dream, but they turn their backs on you suddenly.

These ones go about presenting themselves as the sole supporters of your dream or vision and paint the picture of "what can you do without me?" No one is an island, I quite understand. When God makes you a helper to someone with a mandate or dream, stay committed to the assignment and see God giving you your own dream because of your faithfulness to another man's dream.

HELPERS OF YOUR DREAM

It is important to identify and recognise people whom God has positioned around you to support you as you pray and work hard for your dreams to be fulfilled. These people don't carry name tags by which you can easily identify them. Being sensitive is key to the successful identification of the helpers of your dream. There are three categories of people that I will talk about here.

Committed helper of destiny

This person stays with you in thick and thin to ensure that you do not fail in achieving your God-given dreams. The sayings of others do not bother them. All that matters to them is your success. May God send such people to you and me in Jesus name. Helpers of destiny will leave everything to follow you. They are completely sold out to the fulfilment of your dream. They are not afraid to be number two. They are not envious at all. They are comfortable in their own skin.

Jonathan in 1Samuel 18:3-4 was a committed helper of destiny.

1Samuel 18:3-4

3 Then Jonathan and David made a covenant, because he loved him as his own soul.

4 And Jonathan took off the robe that was on him and gave it to David, with his armor, even to his sword and his bow and his belt.

Spiritual supporter

While you need helpers of destiny for the day-to-day running of your dreams, you also need a set of people to keep the engine of your dream functioning. They are the prayer warriors for your dream. They may not be financially

free to DREAM

available, but they are always on their knees on your behalf praying unto God openly and in secret. We all know that the physical is governed by the spiritual. We need spiritual supporters to stand firm. These people are ready to guide you on how to run with your dream and make a success out of it. They place their hands on you for effectiveness, for synergy and for greater productivity. In 2Kings13: 15-16, Joash the king of Israel enjoyed the spiritual support and guidance of prophet Elisha. Who are the spiritual supporters of your dream? Ask God to send you some.

2 Kings 13:15-16

15 And Elisha said to him, "Take a bow and some arrows." So he took himself a bow and some arrows.

16 Then he said to the king of Israel, "Put your hand on the bow." So he put his hand on it, and Elisha put his hands on the king's hands.

free to DREAM

Encouragers

These people applaud you when you are succeeding and even when you are not making much progress in achieving your dream. They are there cheering you up to go and make it work. They so much believe in you that any temporary failure is seen as part of your growth. They see your fall as a learning curve. They are there not to please you but to please God who sent them to you, working tirelessly and selflessly to see you succeed.

DREAMS COME TRUE

When I was young, I had dreams of a glorious marriage. I desired a marriage where Godly peace and genuine love would be paramount. I wanted a husband that would care for me and our children. I dreamt of a homely and loving husband. My dream family was one where my children would be around me living in abundance of God's provision especially in terms of food and clothing. All these were lacking in my life when I was growing up as a child.

I dreamt of a home and not a house. A home is a safe place for all, but a house is just a place where you are shielded from the elements and not from emotional troubles. There is neither the peace nor the fear of God in some houses. A house is a physical structure while a home is where the love and the Spirit of God dwell. Even when there is scarcity, a home gives you hope

free to DREAM

that the current situation is temporal. You get the re-assurance that this is just a phase in life that will soon pass away. A home is a place where the joy of other family members matters to all.

As a single lady, I dreamt of a home where my husband would come back from work and sit peacefully at the living room reading his newspaper with me sitting beside him and our children playing beside us with glasses of milk to drink. I constantly imagined my house full of different types of good food and ice cream for my children. I remember vividly where I was standing at the Obalende Police barracks where my mother lived at the time. I was not born again but deep in my heart, I knew there was a God in heaven who granted people's innermost heart's desires. He grants your dreams when they are in line with His plan and purpose for your life. The prayer that you pray with your total trust in God receive speedy answers. Do

free to DREAM

you remember the prayer of Hannah the mother of prophet Samuel? The bible says that her lips were moving but her voice was not heard and at some point, Eli thought she was drunk.

Rise up from bowing down your head because of your adversary and pour out your heart to God with whom the solution to all your unfulfilled dreams lie.

1Samuel 1:12-13

12 And it happened, as she continued praying before the Lord, that Eli watched her mouth.

13 Now Hannah spoke in her heart; only her lips moved, but her voice was not heard. Therefore Eli thought she was drunk.

There are times that all you need do is to pray silently and be in tune with God, not being distracted by the negative things that people are saying or have said about you. Hannah

free to DREAM

decided to ignore her troubler Peninnah and took her problem to God, The Solution Provider.

Sometimes you need to stay away from dream killers and vision destroyers to be alone with God. Until she made up her mind to be alone with God and shut out the noises of her enemy and rival, Hannah did not see her dream fulfilled. Which woman would not be dreaming of the day when she would carry her own baby? It is every woman's prayer and dream to be a mother. One way or the other, every woman is a potential mother – biologically, spiritually or by adoption. As a woman, you were created with a womb to give birth to great things and preserve nations born by you or others.

During one of my business trips from Nigeria to London, United Kingdom, I was on the bus travelling to a warehouse in Enfield Lock, North London. I looked out from the bus window and saw school children in their uniform coming out

free to DREAM

of the school with their parents at closing time. There was a strong desire in my mind, that my children would one day be in London with these school children and walking home with me at closing time. That was around 2003. It was something that I sincerely desired and wanted God to do for me. It was my heart's cry to God. I had no idea how it would happen, but I had hope in God.

Two years later in 2005, my family came to the UK for vacation and a year later my family relocated to London UK.

The dream of yesterday has now become today's reality. What is stopping you from dreaming? Do you see yourself as what others said about you? Are you thinking about yourself as a no-good person? It is very important to see yourself in the mirror of God. And what does that mirror reflect? Is says you are fearfully and wonderfully made.

free to DREAM

Psalm 139:14

14 I will praise You, for I am fearfully and wonderfully made;

Marvelous are Your works,

And that my soul knows very well.

What else do you want to hear or see before you pursue your God-given dreams? You are more than who you think you are. I suggest you take another look at yourself and praise the name of God for His loving kindness to you.

My dream became a reality. It became something that was touchable. God gave me tangible proofs. He made it possible for me and my husband to take our children to school in their uniforms just as I had imagined, with plenty of food in the house, milk for teatime with assorted biscuits and ice cream. Is God not great? Please go ahead and dream, and make sure you dream big. Someone says," bite more than you can chew, and God will help you to chew it". What a loaded statement! Remember, even if you decide to bite small bits, it will still take God to help you chew the bits successfully.

See, it does not take God eternity or cost Him anything to bring your dream to come to pass. Only dream the dream that God approves.

I remember when cars with fiberglass body was introduced into Nigeria, it was a big thing to have such cars. These cars came with shinning and beautifully shaped bodies unlike the straight and rectangular shaped cars that were around until then. I would look at these cars and imagine my family having one. Before I knew what was happening, God gave us one such car. My next-door neighbour had gone to a car shop to buy a car. She loved the car and had planned to return the next day to pay for it. When we got to the same car shop later in the day, the asking price for the car was the exact

free to DREAM

money we had with us. If we removed the tithe, the money would not be enough. But knowing that God must be first in all things, our finance inclusive, we took out the tithe and asked God to help us. After much haggling with the car dealer, he accepted our offer which was the balance after the deduction of the tithe. There is nothing God cannot do for you when you are mindful of His kingdom.

Dare to dream and watch patiently as your dreams are fulfilled by the loving hands of God.

Psalms 40:1-3

 I waited patiently for the Lord;

And He inclined to me,

And heard my cry.

2 He also brought me up out of a horrible pit,

Out of the miry clay,

And set my feet upon a rock,

free to DREAM

And established my steps.

3 He has put a new song in my mouth—

Praise to our God;

Many will see it and fear,

And will trust in the Lord.

There is need for patience after you dream. Nothing happens by magic. Note that not all dreams come true especially when it is not in line with God's plan and purpose for His children. No father wants to give a gift that will destroy his child. Instead, he looks for a way to protect and shield his child away from anything that will harm him or her. No matter how much you love your 5-year-old child, you will never give him or her a car key to drive. God loves you and me so much that He would not allow our dream to come to pass if it would destroy us or expose us to danger.

free to DREAM

As a woman or man looking for the perfect man or woman to marry, you must realize that the lady or gentleman that you are eyeing and dreaming of, may not be the man or woman that God has chosen for you. When you dream, invite God into it. Put your own priority on hold and let the things of God be number one in your dream and you will see how God will be mindful of your business, your marriage inclusive. He originated marriage anyway.

Dreaming is powerful especially when it is in line with God's plan. We may not have access to the future now, but we can dream of the future in our minds aligning it with God's will as revealed in His word. The Bible says, "As far as your eyes can see". How far can your physical eyes see? God is not expecting us to break the walls facing us physically, but to see through the walls that separate us from God's plan for

free to DREAM

us. Look beyond limitations and lack. Look above and not beneath. Look ahead and not behind. If you keep looking behind, you are yielding to the power of recession and your forward movement will be impeded. You slow yourself down and this does not glorify God. The word says, "the path of the just is as a shining light that shines brighter and brighter until the perfect day".

Proverbs 4:18

18 But the path of the just is like the shining sun,

That shines ever brighter unto the perfect day.

Dream success and put in your very best to achieve your dreams. If you do not dream about greatness how will you know when greatness comes your way. You either overlook it and pass by it or greatness will pass by you and look for someone else who is expectant and who has dreamt about greatness.

free to DREAM

Expectation is the mother of manifestation according to Bishop David Oyedepo.

I dreamt of living in a place like the UK with my children drinking milk after school and glowing in God's abundance. May I say this. While on a bus in Enfield Lock, some school children came in and sat directly opposite me. I looked at their skins and saw them glowing because of the good weather, the peace of mind they enjoyed, and above all the nourishment from the good food they ate. These children were the same colour as me. Immediately a thought came, that my children could be like these ones if not better. At this time, as I had mentioned, I was a businesswoman, travelling outside my country and my husband had a very good job. That meant we were not doing bad financially. Yet my heart was yearning for something better. Something that was more important than what money could buy for my family. I remember dreaming about living in a place secured enough that I would not be afraid to turn on the light in my home in the middle of the night to study the word of God and to pray to my Heavenly Father. I could not do those things because of lack of security where we were living then. You could hear gun shots in the neighbourhood every night and you hurriedly switched off your lights so armed robbers would not notice that someone was at home or awake. What a terrible experience!

Remember, my dreams were pointing towards my relationship with God and my desire to have a Godly and sound family where peace reigns and God's love abides. I should quickly mention that all these dreams were fuelled by the lack of care that I experienced as a child when I was growing up. I did have a loving father who had the interest of his children at heart but there were some limitations or barriers which prevented him from giving his full love to his children.

free to DREAM

My parents started well in marriage but did not enjoy marital bliss for long. The entrance of a strange woman changed the course of my parents' lives which automatically affected the lives of the only two children (my elder brother, Mr Jibola Lawal and myself) they had then. I started witnessing the physical abuse of my mother. At the slightest opportunity, my father physically abused her everyday. In my subconsciousness as a child under the age of ten, I began to imagine how it would be or feel to live in an atmosphere of love as a family. I started imagining what it meant to be happily married. I started imagining having a home filled with care and love instead of daily violence. I saw my mother being physically abused and would never forget the day the other woman bit my mother's eye. My mother almost lost one eye. Why was this? My father never had a dream or prayed for a loving home where God reigns and rules permanently in his

free to DREAM

marriage. It is very dangerous not to dream ahead of how you want your home to be and ask God to help you live that dream.

I cherish my marriage so much especially my children that I cannot imagine not having them around me. Sometimes I just thank God for keeping me alive because I know where I would have been if not for God's love and mercy. I thank God always for using me as a vessel or vessel through which my children came to this world that is filled with God's love.

I appreciate God for making my dream come true in the choice of the husband he blessed me with. It could have been someone else and that could have caused great pain in my life. A previous two-year deceitful relationship could have made me to miss the plan of God for my life. But God, the Merciful, Loving and Caring Father saved me from pain and misery.

free to DREAM

If I as an unbeliever can experience the great mercies of God, then I believe there are greater mercies in stock for every person that is reading this book. No matter how far you might have gone the wrong way pursuing the wrong dream, God's mercy will find you the same way He found and favoured me.

What is the dream in your heart each time you are alone to imagine things?

One of my heart's desires is to be married in a white wedding dress but I got married in a Yoruba traditional wear. I could not wear the white dress that I had been dreaming about. But when God hears you and sees the sincerity of your dreams, no matter how long or how far, He walks you back to the dream, taking your hand in His to take you to that dream of your future.

My husband proposed to me on a quiet, dusty road in a street in Ilaro Ogun state Nigeria,

free to DREAM

when I was a student. There were no witnesses to shout, "say yes, say yes". There were just two of us and of course the Holy Spirit with the angels even though I was not born again at the time. Your present position matters in what happens in your life but above all is God's grace and mercies. He can turn things around to work for your good even when you do not know Him. Jesus died for us all when we were yet sinners. The blood that was shed on Calvary's tree is for all. No one is excluded, no matter what you believe right now.

Romans 5:8

8 But God demonstrates His own love toward us, in that while we were still sinners, Christ died for us.

The thing is, you must trust God and take a quick journey to know Him and trust Him while His torchlight of grace is still on you. Do not

free to DREAM

delay your surrender to Him. Delay may be costly. When He calls you, answer with speed and allow Him to lead and guide you to His love and truth.

30 years after my husband made his marriage proposal on that quiet dusty road in Nigeria, my God-given children called me at our home in Canada (notice the difference in location. 30 years ago, it was Nigeria, now it is Canada). Please dream and have God at the centre of your dream.

 The children invited me to the living room and said, "we realised that by November, it would be exactly thirty years since daddy proposed to you. I said y--e-e-e-s. Their next statement was, "we have decided to make daddy propose to you in our presence and to renew his vow to you wearing that wedding gown that you have been dreaming about." You can imagine what was going on in my mind. The flash of my dream

free to DREAM

30 years ago suddenly came to life and I was faced with the possibility of living my dream. What a faithful God we serve. He is too faithful and beautiful beyond description. Who or what can you liken Him to? He has no comparison. He is God and God alone.

Hear what the mother of Our Lord Jesus said when she experienced the faithfulness of God:

Luke 1:46-49

46 And Mary said:

"My soul magnifies the Lord,

47 And my spirit has rejoiced in God my Savior.

48 For He has regarded the lowly state of His maidservant;

For behold, henceforth all generations will call me blessed.

free to DREAM

49 For He who is mighty has done great things
for me,

And holy is His name.

My mind greatly magnifies the Lord, the God of the Universe. Nothing can be compared to His mightiness and love. He loves unconditionally. He gives without reproach. He blesses beyond our imagination. He is Love, Love, Love, and Love…

So, 30 years after the first proposal, my husband proposed to me again in the presence of our three children. All of them, now university graduates witnessed the fulfilment of my dream in the presence of God's people.

My husband married me again! Our youngest child handed me over to his dad in marriage. God is a good God. Never allow anyone, or anything to stop you from dreaming. All I would like to advise is that you should dream a Godly dream. Dream the dream that aligns with God's

free to DREAM

eternal agenda. Dream to be a source of blessing to many. Never dream of causing pain to anyone. If you dream negative dreams, you only get negative outcomes. Be positive in your dreams so positive and great things can happen to you.

free to DREAM

A FINAL WORD

God allowed my dreams to be fulfilled and I am still waiting for other dreams to come true. God does not disappoint. Remember, when I was having some of those dreams, I was not born again; I only had a ray of light that there was God somewhere. John spoke about an amount of light in everyone created by God in whose nostrils is the life of God.

John1:4/9

4 In Him was life, and the life was the light of men.

9 That was the true Light which gives light to every man coming into the world.

There is no one on earth without God's spirit because His breath (Spirit) was released on His creatures to make them be like Him.

Please acknowledge the Lordship of God in your life by making Him matter in all your situation.

free to DREAM

It is only God who can make dreams to come true.

Remember that a selfish dream is not a Godly dream.

Dubai and Abu Dhabi were once unknown communities in the open desert. They were unappealing and undesirable, but through the dream of someone or a group of people they became places that everyone now wants to visit. A dream transformed the cities into commercial centres for the nation and the entire region and a source of pride to the inhabitants.

Walt Disney started as a dream in the mind of its owner. See what it has become! High rise buildings, aircrafts, computers, new IT technologies and many other successful businesses started as dreams in the minds of people.

What is your own dream?

free to DREAM

Will the dream benefit others?

Will the dream be allowed to come to life?

The answers to these questions lie within you.

Let me borrow some words from Martin Luther King:

"I have a dream that one day this nation will rise up and live out the true meaning of its creed: "We hold these truths to be self-evident; that all men are created equal.

I have a dream that one day on the red hills of Georgia the sons of former slaves and the sons of former slave owners will be able to sit down together at the table of brotherhood".

You are free to dream but when you dream, never give up on your dream.

He revealed hidden dreams to Daniel and brought them to pass.

Daniel 2:27-28

free to DREAM

27 Daniel answered in the presence of the king, and said, "The secret which the king has demanded, the wise men, the astrologers, the magicians, and the soothsayers cannot declare to the king.

 28 But there is a God in heaven who reveals secrets, and He has made known to King Nebuchadnezzar what will be in the latter days. Your dream, and the visions of your head upon your bed, were these:

Why not make that great confession with your mouth declaring God's name and power because with your mouth, confessing is made unto Salvation.

Romans 10:10

10 For with the heart one believes unto righteousness, and with the mouth confession is made unto salvation.

free to DREAM

Decide to invite Jesus Christ into your dreams today by saying these words loudly with an open heart:

Lord Jesus, I come to you today I confess that I am a sinner.

I ask for the forgiveness of my sins and invite you to be my Lord and Savour.

Wash me clean with Your blood that was shed on Calvary's tree.

I believe you died for me and my sins. You rose up on the third day and set me free.

From now on, I declare You as my personal Lord and Saviour,

Thank You Lord for saving me. I am free, I am born again, I am a child of God.

Thank You Jesus. Amen.

I believe you said that prayer with your heart and meant every word of it. Welcome to a life

free to DREAM

full of God's mercies and favour. A life where Godly dreams are being fulfilled by the resurrection power of Christ.

A life of hope and love.

A life that is meaningful.

Congratulations.

There is no fear in Christ Jesus. So, dare to dream and be expectant that your dreams will come true.

 I dreamt to live in a place or country where I could pray to God at midnight and study the word of God at night with lights on without the fear of armed robbers and God relocated my family.

I dreamt of a Godly and caring husband and God did it.

I dreamt of my children schooling in the UK and God made it to happen.

free to DREAM

I dreamt about wearing a white wedding gown and God made it to be after 30 years. God is not restrained or constrained by time. He created time and the seasons (Genesis 1). He controls all of life's affairs. Age is not a barrier for God to showcase His love and promises. He is the Ancient of Days.

Abraham the father of faith became a father at age 90. How old are you that you are giving up on your dreams? Dream big and achieve your God-given dreams. It is never too late.

There is no age or time limit for your dreams to be fulfilled. Time and season are in the Hands of God. He is not restricted by time; He controls the time. The time of the fulfilment of your dream is in His hands and He makes all things beautiful in His time. The bible says, that there is an appointed time for the vision but it will speak when it is time.

Habakkuk 2:3

free to DREAM

For the vision is yet for an appointed time;

But at the end it will speak, and it will not lie.

Though it tarries, wait for it;

Because it will surely come,

It will not tarry.

It may seem as if others have gone ahead of you in the journey of life, never allow that to bother you. When it is your time of favour, God will put springs on your heels that will make your steps be with springs and your journey faster and better. He made prophet Elijah to outrun the chariot of the king. He will make you overtake those that you think have gone ahead of you in Jesus name.

1 Kings18:46

free to DREAM

46 Then the hand of the Lord came upon Elijah; and he girded up his loins and ran ahead of Ahab to the entrance of Jezreel.

It takes God's Hands to fulfil dreams and to make available the strength you need for the fulfilment of the dream.

I grew up in an environment that was so hash to the point that, there was no mattress for me to sleep on in the house anytime I went home on school breaks even as a college student just because of strange women in my father's life.

The first time I had a bed I could call my own was in high school because of hostel policies. You had no other option than to have your own mattress.

No situation is permanent when your hopes and dreams are in line with God's plan for your life.

Keep dreaming and achieving great and mighty things.

free to DREAM

Nothing is high or low enough to stop your God-given dream. The pit into which Joseph's brothers dropped him because of their hatred for him could not stop his dream. The prison where he served his jail term because of a false accusation by Potiphar's wife could not hold him back from his dream. In fact, those challenges were the ladders that he climbed to greatness in a foreign land. Here is a slave becoming the Prime Minister of a nation where he was neither born nor known.

Genesis chapters 39 and 40.

Shake off any weight or barrier that may be hindering your dream from being fulfilled. Walk tall and keep moving without looking back or answering any of your critics.

You are destined for greatness.

You are blessed in Jesus Name.

Amen.

free to DREAM

free to DREAM

free to DREAM

Other Books by Titilayo Akinniyi

free to DREAM

www.ingramcontent.com/pod-product-compliance
Lightning Source LLC
Chambersburg PA
CBHW021344060726
47591CB00006B/2153